The *Life*
Your *Spirit*
Craves

30 DAY DEVOTIONAL AND JOURNAL

Acknowledgements

I would like to thank my Lord and Savior, Jesus Christ for loving me and entrusting me with such a task. May your name receive all the praise.

Special thank you to my husband who has been very loving and supportive.

My baby girl, Eden for understanding that she needed to go to bed extra early sometimes so that mommy could write.

My mom, dad, stepdad, sisters and extended family.

Nickole Byrd and Cynthia Patterson for their words of wisdom throughout my writing and publishing process.

My editor Erin Mercer.

My photographer Chanell Shorter, ShortEr Photography.

My graphic designer Earl Duncan (thank you for your patience).

My friends who listened to me and provided candid feedback.

Pastor Larry Benford and the Living Word Fellowship Church family.

Pastor Terrance Johnson and the Higher Dimension Church family.

Foreword

Every now and then a book will come along and shake the Christian landscape to its core. Such a book has arrived. Not only does this book challenge it's readers with intense bible study it also moves one to life application. When you think of a daily devotional, you would not ordinarily think of or expect intensity. Quite the surprise at first glance! You are moved to think!

The daily scriptures are prayerfully well thought out and strategically placed to ensure that the reader will achieve a total bible experience, unlike most devotionals which focus on only portions of the conans. Having over forty years as a Christian who desires a more intimate and personal relationship with the Savior, I highly recommend this book as a daily tool to assist in reaching new spiritual heights.

Pastor Larry Benford
Living Word Fellowship Church, Greenville, MS

From the Author's Heart

Before delving into the pages of this book, I would like you to take a moment to think about a few things. Think about what you desire most out of life. Think about your passion. Think about the most effective ways that you can give to others. Write down your thoughts and review them at the end of this book.

As you read this book, commit to fasting, journaling and praying consistently for the next 30 days. Pray and decide within yourself what you should fast from.

This book was written for the reader who is ready to seek, accept and pursue his/her purpose in life. I believe that each one of us has been created with a purpose in mind. Everyone's purpose is to please God. We please God when we love Him and love one another. The question we should each ask ourselves is "What has God planted in me that will give His name glory and uplift His people?"

There is something within you that will benefit someone else and cause them to be better. You should be positively touching the lives of those around you. Your life matters. You matter. You were created for a divine purpose. Know that "purpose" doesn't mean that you were created to do just one particular thing. Your purpose is a culmination of many assignments and as you read through this book, the question that you are to ask yourself is, "What should I be doing now?" Since this journey is personal to each reader, the prayers and Life Questions are written in first person. As you read and write in the journal, the questions are meant to have you think about where you are in your spiritual journey and reflect on what God is calling you to do at this time in your life.

The title of this book, The Life Your Spirit Craves, derives from the thought that once you accept salvation, your spirit craves the things of God. Since you believe in Christ, your spirit desires to be like Christ and to live the way God has called you to live—according to His purpose!

At the end of this thirty day devotional, it is my prayer that you

- Are walking closer to God and have greater clarity as to what your assignment is at this time in your life,
- Are better equipped to hear God's voice,
- Would have allowed the Holy Spirit to speak, guide and show you how you can best live out the love of God that has been planted within you.

It is never too late to begin living on purpose! Now is the time to live the life you were destined to live!

CONTENTS

SEEKING

ACCEPTING

PURSUING

DAY 1 - Your Purpose Has Been Predetermined

Isaiah 45:4 NLT
"And why have I called you for this work? Why did I call you by name when you did not know me? It is for the sake of Jacob my servant, Israel my chosen one."

Isaiah 45 teaches us that Cyrus was chosen by the Lord to restore his city and free the Lord's people. Cyrus was chosen before he even knew the Lord (v.4). This confirms that your purpose --your destiny-- is predetermined before you meet the Lord, decide to follow Him and give your life over to His purpose.

Verse 2 tells how the Lord will go before Cyrus to help him accomplish his pre-ordained purpose. In verses 9-12, the Bible teaches that you should not argue or question the Lord about why you have been given the assignment in which He purposed for you. The Lord himself will guide your actions (v. 12) and that is assurance enough.

Oftentimes, God may not reveal why He has chosen you for a specific task, especially when the task doesn't line up with your background or education. When this is the case, you have to truly rely on God's power and guidance in order to carry out the assignments that He has pre-ordained for you. I think this serves as a great example of how God sees and knows the strengths within you that you sometimes do not realize you possess. The scripture reveals that God will go before you; you just have to follow. Remember that the assignment on your life is meant to fulfill God's purpose, give God glory and encourage His people.

So in this moment, I encourage you to seek the Lord for your predetermined purpose. Secondly, accept your purpose. Don't question or argue with the Lord about *what* He has called you to do or *why* He has called *you* to do it. No assignment is too big or too small. Receive the Lord's guidance and instruction because he already has the master plan.

Prayer for Today: Lord, I thank you for your greatness and your sovereignty. Lord, I thank you for your purpose for my life. I thank you because you had a plan and purpose for my life even before I knew you. I seek you today so that you may speak to my heart. I want to know you more and what you have purposed for me. Thank you for choosing me. Help me to serve you with joy and boldness. In Jesus' name, Amen.

For further study, please read Isaiah 45:1-13.

DAY 1

JOURNAL

Life Questions/Application

1. For what purpose has the Lord called me?

2. Have I accepted this purpose for my life?

3. What can I do today that will help me to be more faithful to this purpose?

DAY 2 – Ask. Seek. Knock.

Matthew 7:7-8 NLT

Keep on asking, and you will receive what you ask for. Keep on seeking, and you will find. Keep on knocking, and the door will be opened to you. For everyone who asks, receives. Everyone who seeks, finds. And to everyone who knocks, the door will be opened.

Do you know your calling?
Do you know your purpose in the kingdom of God?
Have you even begun seeking God about it?

If not, now is a good time to start. The scripture tells us that when we ask something of the Lord, He will answer. Sometimes, the answer may not be immediate; that is why I believe the scripture says to keep on knocking and the door will be opened. Not only will God answer your prayer, He will open up many doors of opportunity for you to serve in His kingdom, allow you to serve His people and prepare you to be a blessing to them.

I heard a sermon by Pastor Charles Jenkins that discussed "purpose" and "calling." He shared something during his message that I now want to share with you. There are two callings on our lives: corporate and individual. He explained that we must first accept and support the corporate calling—the calling on our church body. (What vision has God given your pastor for the ministry?) The individual calling is the specific calling that God has placed over each one of our lives to build up the kingdom and bring glory to God. God has placed you and I in our respective congregations for purpose. This purpose will support the vision that God has given to our leadership and further the ministry. You are not attending your church by accident!

Before I accepted my assignment and calling to encourage others through the Word of God in writing, I would become very nervous and anxious whenever our pastor (or anyone) would even mention the words "purpose" or "calling." Now, I get excited about hearing messages regarding this topic because I am invigorated!

If you do not know your calling, I encourage you to take the following steps to begin this journey:

1. Accept the corporate calling. This is done by supporting the vision of the ministry through time and finances.
2. Seek the Lord to show you the calling that He has placed on your life. Pray. Study the Word of God. Fast. Consider what you are passionate about. I believe that passion = purpose.

No matter where you are in life, be encouraged and know that it is never too late to do what God has called you to do! Ask. Seek. Knock.

Prayer for Today: Father I thank you for being omniscient and sovereign! I magnify your name. I thank you that you created the purpose for my life even before you created me! I thank you right now for all that you're going to do through my life. I pray that you show me what you want me to do and give me the courage to do it. I thank you for the manifestation of your power in my life, oh Lord! You are awesome and welcome to dwell within me. In Jesus' name, Amen.

For further study, please read Deuteronomy 6:18 and 2 Chronicles 15:2.

DAY 2

JOURNAL

Life Questions/Application

1. What is the corporate calling of the ministry that I belong to?
   a. How have I supported the vision?
   b. What are ways that I can help further the vision of the ministry?

2. Lord please show me opportunities to serve in Your Kingdom. Help me to identify where you can use me and where I can be of service to You. Where is God calling me to serve Him?

DAY 3 - Passion is Purpose

Isaiah 55:8 NLT
"My thoughts are nothing like your thoughts," says the Lord. "And my ways are far beyond anything you could imagine."

I had a heartfelt conversation with a dear friend who is at a crossroad in life. Throughout our time in college, it was well-known to me and many others where her passion lied and what her dreams were. Well, she made several attempts to achieve her dreams and was unsuccessful. Since she did not reach her dreams in *her* self-imposed timeframe, she decided to take a safe route that would get her in the neighborhood but not at her "address" (as my pastor would say). In addition to this, she has placed an immense amount of pressure on herself in other areas of her life and is now wondering what her next steps should be.

As the Holy Spirit whispered this scripture into my spirit, I thought of my friend and our discussion. I was reminded of something that I'd like to share with you: When you're chasing your dream and you experience road blocks, don't give up. Continue to follow your true passion because your passion is the manifestation of your purpose-which comes from God. Distractions and challenges are inevitable. You must identify them, learn from them and keep pressing forward.

She asked me what she should do at this point. Of course my response was to study God's word and pray for direction. I suggested that she find a quiet place to spend quality time with the Lord. He will surely speak to you when you are truly ready to listen and obey!

My friend's next question was: How will I know its God's voice and not my own? The word of God says that "my sheep know my voice." (**John 10:4**) You learn God's voice by spending time studying His word. God will not tell you anything that is not in alignment with the scriptures. (If what you're hearing is contrary to the word of God then it isn't God) In addition, God will always confirm His answer to your prayers.

I encourage you to seek the Lord with all your heart. Be diligent. Remember today's focal scripture. Do not get so far removed from God that you cannot discern His voice and follow His way. His thoughts and ways are different from yours. Even when it seems like it is taking longer than expected to accomplish your goal, there is a lesson to be learned during the rough patches that will better prepare you for where you're going. Just because there is delay or a pause, doesn't mean that it won't happen. Don't give up! God's plan will be carried out!

Prayer for Today: Father in heaven, thank you for your power and your wisdom. Cleanse my heart and mind so that I may clearly hear your voice and determine where you would have me to go. I desire what you want for my life. Teach me to delight in your will and in your ways. In Jesus' name, Amen.

For further study, read John 10 in its entirety.

DAY 3

JOURNAL

Life Questions/Application

1. What am I passionate about? What do I like to spend my time doing? How can I channel this passion to further God's kingdom?

2. Have I been spending time in God's Word so that I may be able to hear His voice? What is God saying to me? If not, what can I change in my life that will allow me to seek the Lord diligently?

3. Am I obeying God's instructions for my life? If not, why am I not obeying God? What obstacles are in my way?

DAY 4 - SPIRITUAL COUNSEL

Proverbs 11:14 NLT
Without wise leadership, a nation falls; there is safety in having many advisers.

Do you have any spiritual mentors? Do you have anyone who you trust and from whom you can seek Godly wisdom?

When you're trying to better yourself and seek to become all God has created you to become, the bible teaches that you need to seek wise counsel. Just as a nation will fall without having wise leadership, so will you. Secure wise mentors for different areas of your life from financial guidance to career and spiritual guidance.

Before you seek counsel, first determine the direction you're headed. Determine your direction by seeking the Lord and receiving wisdom. (Where are you going? What is your plan to get there?) Counselors and advisors are not supposed to tell you what to do. Their role is to help you get to your destination.

Proverbs 16:22 NLT states "plans go wrong for lack of advice; many advisers bring success." In the book of Proverbs, Solomon repeatedly advises to seek wise counsel. Once you determine your direction and make plans to get there, you will obtain success by seeking wise counsel. Seek out mentors who are trustworthy and who may have already accomplished what you're trying to accomplish. I think that you should have at least two people who support you and the vision that God gave you. Mentors do not necessarily have to be older people either. Age is not synonymous with wisdom.

How do you know when you've selected the right persons to mentor you? They will only confirm what God has already told you through prayer and studying His word. Their advice will not contradict God's word.

Prayer for Today: In the name of Jesus, Lord I come to you with praise. I praise you with everything that is within me! I thank you for being who you are! In the name of Jesus, cleanse me, purify me and forgive me of my sins. I believe by faith that I have been forgiven. I ask that you give me wisdom. Give me direction. Help me to find wise counselors who may help me attain safety and success. I only want to go where you want me to go. I only want to do what will bring you joy. In Jesus' name, Amen.

For further study, please read 1 Kings 12:8-16 and Exodus 18:17-23

DAY 4

JOURNAL

Life Questions/Applications

1. Are there any people in my life (church, community, work) whom I trust and can provide spiritual advice? Name them. Are any of these people a mentor to me?

2. I will ask _____ to mentor me and assist me in getting to where God is calling me to be. I will discuss the plans God has for my life and how I believe he/she will assist me in this purpose.

DAY 5 - Heart Check-Up

Proverbs 15:11 NLT
Even Death and Destruction hold no secrets from the Lord. How much more does he know the human heart!

Self-examination: What is the condition of your heart? As often as possible, you should perform self-examinations to learn the condition of your heart.

Proverbs 4:23 teaches that out of the heart, flows the issues of life. The way you walk, talk and speak is a direct reflection of what's in your heart. See **Luke 6:45**.

Once you perform a self-examination, you must come to the realization that God already knows your heart. You must not dwell in all of the things that you've done wrong and have a pity party. No! Seek the Lord because He can create within you a clean heart. See **Psalm 51**.

When you realize that God already knows your heart and you seek his forgiveness, you must turn away from your sin. You cannot allow sin to damage your heart time and time again (which in turn damages your daily life). Let those things go! Change starts with a made up mind and then in your heart. You cannot be pleasing to God if your heart isn't right. Why not? Your actions (thoughts and deeds) are an outward manifestation of what's inside of your heart. God isn't pleased when your ways are not in alignment with His will.

Proverbs 16:7 NLT states "when people's lives please the Lord, even their enemies are at peace with them." Getting your heart right and pleasing God will prove beneficial to you not only spiritually but in day-to-day life as well. Resolve to keep your heart spiritually healthy so that you may live a life pleasing to God and experience the abundant life that you were destined to live.

***Prayer for Today*:** Father in the name of Jesus, I come to you today with a heart filled with praise! You are the Most High God! Hallelujah! You're worthy of all of my praise and I give it to you today Father! Lord I ask that you forgive me of my sins. Take an inventory of my heart. Remove everything that's not like you. Purify me. Help me to turn away and never return to those things that do not please you. Help me to remain steadfast in your Word and in your Way. Let me purpose in my heart to remain diligent and seek to become more and more like you each day. I know it's not easy but it's worth it! I love you and honor you today. Thank you for loving me so much that you sent your only son Jesus to die for my sins! As I go about my day today, let my heart be sensitive to your voice so that before I even think, say or do anything contrary to your will, you will remind me of who I am in you! In Jesus' name, Amen.

For further study, please read Proverbs 16:2, Luke 6:45 and Psalm 51.

DAY 5

JOURNAL

Life Questions/Application

1. When is the last time I performed a self-examination and allowed the Lord to search my heart?

2. The things in my life that I know are not pleasing to the Lord are

3. What does God's word say about these things?

DAY 6 - BEING A LEADER

Proverbs 12:24 NLT
Work hard and become a leader; be lazy and become a slave.

Last year, I read this book titled, "You Don't Need a Title to Be a Leader," by Mark Sanborn. The book gives several examples of people who worked very hard but did not have accompanying titles that matched their level of contribution to their respective organizations.. These people were not managers or CEOs. These people weren't even working hard because they wanted a title. Their great work ethic was part of their character. They loved their jobs and each had a passion for what they were doing each day.

Many of these people came up with ways to improve efficiency, increase morale and boost productivity. Eventually, many of the people mentioned in Mr. Sanborn's book received the "title" to match their contributions. However, that was not their purpose for being great at their jobs; they simply wanted to make things better. They weren't looking for special recognition.

Many times we do something "special" at work or church to gain recognition or to get "an edge" over the next person. When the outcome is not as expected, we're upset because the actions did not come from a pure heart! Make sure that whatever you're doing, you're pursuing it for the right reasons. Do everything unto God; He is the rewarder of your efforts. He will open up doors of opportunity for you when you're pleasing Him!

Today I encourage you to work hard regardless of your title. **Proverbs 13:4 NLT says** *"Lazy people want much but get little, but those who work hard will prosper."*

Work hard because that's who you are. Work hard because you are working unto God. Work hard because this pleases God and you're seeking to become who He has created you to be.

So even though it may seem like no one sees your hard work, God sees it! He will promote you in His timing! Your hard work will pay off in due season and you will reap your harvest if you faint not. **(See Galatians 6:9)**

Prayer for Today: Father, in the mighty and powerful name of Jesus, I honor and praise your Holy name! I come to pour out my thanksgiving and praise on you today. I ask that you forgive me of my sins and make me more like you. I ask that you give me the strength to continue to work hard even when I haven't received elevation. Change my heart so that working hard will be who I am because I desire to please you! Help me to do all things unto you so that you may receive all the glory, honor and most high praise! In Jesus' name, Amen!

For further study, please read 2 Chronicles 19:5-7, Galatians 6:9 and Matthew 20:26-28

DAY 6

JOURNAL

Life Questions/Application

1. For what reason(s) do I work hard? Am I working hard to please others or please the Lord? Am I seeking recognition from someone other than God? Am I working hard so that I can bring glory to the Lord?

2. How can I be sure that my motives are pure? What can I start doing today that will assure me that I am consistent and my heart is in the right place?

3. Am I pursuing my purpose to please those around me or the Lord? How can I be sure?

DAY 7 - Waiting For Your Dream to Be Fulfilled

Matthew 2:15 NLT
"and they stayed there until Herod's death. This fulfilled what the Lord had spoken through the prophet: "I called my Son out of Egypt."

Matthew 2:17 NLT
" Herod's brutal action fulfilled what God had spoken through the prophet Jeremiah:"

Matthew 2:22 NLT
"So the family went and lived in a town called Nazareth. This fulfilled what the prophets had said."

What has God promised you?
What dream has He spoken into your heart?
What Word is he constantly speaking to you through His messenger (your pastor)?

In the scripture references above, things that the prophets spoke about Jesus were beginning to happen just as they said. This is important because the prophet's words came from God and they were fulfilled. Everything that God has spoken about you will be fulfilled as well.

During this journey, you are to seek God to see what lies in your destiny. You are to see what God says about you and what He has called you to do. You can only do that by spending time in His Word and communicating with Him through prayer.

Take some time to think about the sermons you've heard over the past three months. More likely than not, there has been a consistent message that God has been speaking and trying to get through to you. Generally, I find that when there is a question on my heart, God answers it many times through His Word, my pastor, other people or circumstances. Each time, the answer is the same. I mention this because I want to point out that God is constantly speaking to you. He is consistent. He confirms His word over and over again. He is forever showing you that your path has already been prepared for you; you just have to be obedient and walk in it.

The project of writing and publishing books (especially this book) has been on my heart for several years now. Over the past several months, I began to pray and ask God for direction. He answered my prayer through His Word, dreams, sermons from my pastor and through an evangelist on TV that I wasn't even watching!

I share this with you to encourage you. When God puts something in your heart, you will not be able to let it go. You will not rest until it is done. It will continue to resurface in your heart and mind time and time again. Know that the assignments you've been given are for God's glory and not your own. God's plans will be accomplished even if He has to reassign them!

Now if you're already aware of what God is calling you to do, stay focused on your walk towards destiny! Whatever message that is being constantly spoken into you will be fulfilled. God's word will not return unto Him void (Isaiah 55:11). It will certainly accomplish the purpose for which it was sent.

Prayer for Today: Father God, you are most Holy and kind to me. Thank you for your compassion and mercy. Lord, I ask that you continue to speak to my heart. Empower and encourage me through your word so that I may continue to walk in destiny and fulfill what you have predestined for me in this life. In Jesus' name, Amen.

For further study, please read Matthew 2 and Isaiah 55.

DAY 7

JOURNAL

Life Questions/Application

1. Can I identify a particular message that I've been hearing over the past few months?
   a. What is that message?
   b. How does it apply to me?
   c. What is God asking me to do?

2. How can I begin to apply this message to my life today?

DAY 8 - "Eat What You Have First"

Matthew 25:23 NLT
"The master said, 'Well done, my good and faithful servant. You have been faithful in handling this small amount, so now I will give you many more responsibilities. Let's celebrate together!'

In my youth, whenever my mom would cook something that I really enjoyed (usually chicken) I would always ask for more before I started eating. Her response to me would always be "eat what you have first."

As I ponder that statement, I think about how many of us ask God for more strength or courage to accomplish our goals when the truth is that we were given everything we needed to complete the assignment before we were even aware of the assignment. The issue is that we haven't even began to use or tap into those things so we do not know what we have. We do not understand that we are already "full." We use "waiting on God to answer our prayers" as an excuse to procrastinate.

Today I encourage you to use what God has already given you. You are already equipped! How do you know that you do not have what you need to accomplish your goal if you haven't tapped into it? How do you know that you do not already have the right tools if you haven't even started working towards accomplishing your goal?

You will waste valuable time asking God for what He has already given you and then sitting around waiting for it. This is a clever tactic of the enemy. See, when you believe that you don't have what you need, you are fearful. When you are fearful, you are not moving toward your destiny but simply in the opposite direction. Take hold of what God has already placed in you and use it! Eat what you have first and then ask for more. Be faithful over a few things (what you've already been given). God will make you ruler over many. **(See Matthew 25:21)**

Prayer for Today: Father in Heaven, through my Lord and Savior Jesus Christ, I come to you giving you glory and magnifying your name. Thank you for your faithfulness and kindness. Thank you for all that you've placed within me to fulfill my assignments. I ask that you search me and reveal unto me those things that you've given me to reach my destiny. Give me wisdom and courage to use the tools that you've already equipped me with. Let me not make excuses and procrastinate, but move forward in your calling for my life. In Jesus' name, Amen.

For further study, please read Matthew 25:14-30, Psalm 18:24-26 and Psalm 65:4-6.

DAY 8

JOURNAL

Life Questions/Application

1. Have I been procrastinating in fulfilling God's purpose for my life? Why?

2. What tools have God already provided to assist me in walking in my destiny?

3. Am I clear on God's calling on my life? What is it?

DAY 9 - Character

Psalm 105:19 NLT
Until the time came to fulfill his dreams, the Lord tested Joseph's character.

Many times when God places dreams in your heart and you purpose in your heart to fulfill it, you will encounter many obstacles along the way. Today's scripture enlightens us to the fact that the Lord is the one who tested Joseph's character before his dreams came to pass. Do you remember all of the things that Joseph encountered before his dreams were fulfilled?

Let us first recount Joseph's dreams. His first dream *(Genesis 37:6) is that he is in a field with his brothers, tying up bundles of grain. Suddenly his bundle stood up, and his brothers' bundles all gathered around and bowed low before his.* His second dream *(Genesis 37:9) was that the sun, moon, and even stars bowed low before him!* These dreams signified that Joseph would be ruler.

Let us revisit the obstacles he encountered before his dreams came to past. First, his brothers sold him into slavery. (Even as a slave to Potiphar, God was with him and still gave him success in everything that he did). Second, Joseph was put in prison because Potiphar's wife lied on him. (Still the Lord was with Joseph in prison and made him a favorite with the prison warden.)

One day, Joseph was called upon to interpret Pharaoh's dream. After Joseph interpreted Pharaoh's dream, Pharaoh put Joseph in charge of the entire land of Egypt! Dream fulfilled! Joseph became ruler just as his dreams indicated!

No matter what obstacles you are facing, remember that they are just stepping stones to get you where you need to be. They are just a testing of your character. The obstacles will only sharpen and prepare you for when the time comes for your dream(s) to be fulfilled.

I imagine that Joseph became more patient throughout the process and even developed a better relationship with God seeing as how God continued to give him success even when his circumstances weren't that great! I imagine that this caused Joseph to give God even more praise and worship! Joseph gave credit to God for everything that had happened. **Genesis 45:5-8 NLT states** *"But don't be upset, and don't be angry with yourselves for selling me to this place. It was God who sent me here ahead of you to preserve your lives. This famine that has ravaged the land for two years will last five more years, and there will be neither plowing nor harvesting. God has sent me ahead of you to keep you and your families alive and to preserve many survivors. So it was God who sent me here, not you! And he is the one who made me an adviser to Pharaoh-the manager of his entire palace and the governor of all of Egypt!"*

Today if you're encountering difficulties while working toward fulfilling your God-given dream, remember that the obstacles are only a testing of your character and you will benefit from the experiences! God's plans are for your good and to give you hope and a future. **(Read Jeremiah 29:11)**

Prayer for Today: Father in heaven, I honor and praise your holy name today! You are Most worthy of all of my praise! Sustain me during the times when my character is being tested. Give me strength and help me to not lose sight of what you have in store for me. Things that I can't even imagine! You are so great to me and your faithful love endures forever and ever! In Jesus' name, please be my strength, Amen.

For further study, please read Genesis 37, Joshua 1:1-9 and Jeremiah 29:11.

DAY 9

JOURNAL

Life Questions/Application

1. What tests (or difficulties) am I currently encountering?
    a. Am I allowing these obstacles to take my focus off my goals?
    b. Am I using the obstacles as a way to grow closer to God?

2. How can I use my obstacles as opportunities for growth?

DAY 10 – Work While You Wait

Habakkuk 2:3 NLT
For the revelation awaits an appointed time; it speaks of the end and will not prove false. Though it linger, wait for it; it will certainly come and will not delay.

Whatever the vision, goal or dream that God has planted in your heart will come to pass. God will not give you a dream or vision that He has not already equipped you for. He has not placed anything within you that you cannot attain.

As you wait for the appointed time for your dream to come to pass, I'd like to encourage you to work while you wait. Prepare for it! Write down your plan (v.2) and put it in a place where it will constantly be before you. Put it on the refrigerator. Place it in your bible. Tape it to the dashboard of your car. Position yourself by preparing yourself so that you may be ready when the opportunity arises. Work diligently to attain your goal.

Proverbs 13:4 NLT says *"The sluggard craves and gets nothing but the desires of the diligent are fully satisfied."* To be diligent means to constantly work at something; not give up. Diligent people do not take "no" for an answer. They are persistent and consistent because they are highly motivated. They know that if they don't work for it, they won't get it.

Proverbs 10:4 NLT says *"Lazy hands make a man poor, but diligent hands bring wealth."* Whatever it is that you are trying to achieve will not happen on its own. God gave you the vision for a purpose. He wants you to work for it. If He said that it is going to happen, it will happen, but you also have to do what is required of you to accomplish it.

Seek God for what He wants you to do. Next, write down the vision and plan that you have been given and put them in a place where they will constantly be before you. Then, work toward accomplishing this goal while you wait on the Lord Jesus to make the right opportunities available. If you need something to take your mind off the wait while you're working, keep a song on your heart. The ministry of music is a blessing to your soul. Keep a positive attitude while working.

Prayer for Today: Father God I come to you in the holy and powerful name of Jesus seeking your will for my life. I pray that you speak to me like never before and just breathe your purpose into my heart. Give me understanding and wisdom so that I may seek after that which you have called me. Help me to stay focused and walk in your purpose for my life. In Jesus' name, Amen.

For further study, please read Habbakuk 2:1-5 and Psalm 32:6-8

DAY 10

JOURNAL

Life Questions/Application

1. What am I doing to seek God for what He wants me to do?

2. Have I written down the vision? Have I drafted a plan to accomplish this?

3. Commit to drafting a plan. I am going to put it - _____ where I will see it daily to remind myself of what I am working toward.

DAY 11 - Obedience

1 Samuel 15:16-20 NLT

Then Samuel said to Saul, "Stop! Listen to what the Lord told me last night!"

"What did he tell you?" Saul asked.

And Samuel told him, "Although you may think little of yourself, are you not the leader of the tribes of Israel? The Lord has anointed you king of Israel. And the Lord sent you on a mission and told you, 'Go and completely destroy the sinners, the Amalekites, until they are all dead.' Why haven't you obeyed the Lord? Why did you rush for the plunder and do what was evil in the Lord's sight?"

"But I did obey the Lord," Saul insisted. "I carried out the mission he gave me. I brought back King Agag, but I destroyed everyone else.

In this passage, Samuel was basically calling Saul out on his sin. Saul did not fully obey the Lord when the Lord instructed him to destroy the Amalekites. Saul saved King Agag (King of Amalekites) and the best of the cattle, sheep, goats, and other animals. He only destroyed what *he thought* was worthless. The Lord became angry with Saul and rejected him. The Lord then chose someone else (David) to be king. Saul's disobedience caused him to lose his blessing (position and favor) with God. I think this is a good example of how our disobedience can cause us to lose out on our blessings.

How many blessings have you missed out on or lost because of sin and disobedience?

When God gives you instructions, whether through prayer, studying his word or through your pastor, you must be careful to do exactly what He has told you to do. In today's meditational passage, Samuel told Saul what the Lord had spoken to him. *"Saul was chosen as leader. Saul was the anointed king of Israel. The Lord sent Saul. The Lord told Saul. Why didn't Saul obeyed the Lord? Why did Saul rush for the plunder and do what was evil in the Lord's sight?"* Notice that instructions were given directly to Saul regarding his assignment. Yet, Saul didn't do all that the Lord asked. Partial obedience is still disobedience.

God gives the instruction to you so you are responsible for your actions. You cannot blame your sins and disobedience on others. Do not miss out on the greatness of God because of selfish ambition! God wants the best for you.

Samuel goes on to say in verse 22 that obedience is better than sacrifice! Saul's excuse for his sin was that he was going to use what he didn't destroy as burnt offering and sacrifice to the Lord. The Lord prefers obedience!

So today, ask the Lord to examine your heart. Repent for your times of disobedience and resolve to be obedient to God's word today and hereafter. Resolve to do everything that God has called you to do. You are held responsible once you receive God's message!

Prayer for Today: Oh Most Holy and Most High God! I reverence your Holy name! Thank you for your righteousness and your Word that guides me! In the name of Jesus, forgive me for my sins. Teach me to walk in the right paths. I submit my will to yours today and ask that you lead me in the paths of righteousness for your name sake. Thank you for your presence. Thank you for loving and accepting me. In Jesus' name, Amen.

For further study, please read Deuteronomy 28 and 1 Samuel 15 in their entirety.

DAY 11

JOURNAL

Life Questions/Application

1. What instructions have God given me to fulfill my God-given assignment in this season of my life? Have I fully obeyed His instructions?

2. Lord examine me and show me the areas where I have not been fully obedient to your instructions.
   a. The Lord has revealed to me that I have not been fully obedient when He instructed me to

DAY 12 - Filter

Isaiah 30:21 NLT
Your own ears will hear him. Right behind you a voice
will say, "This is the way you should go," whether to the
right or to the left.

Earlier in this chapter, Judah sought help from Egypt,
contrary to God's plan for them. This chapter teaches us
that seeking help from anyone other than the Lord will lead
to destruction (v.12 -15). We will only experience lasting
success and peace when we seek the Lord and follow the
instructions of His voice.

Have you ever been faced with such a big decision that
you've talked it over with everyone but God? Well, I'm
guilty of that. I remember being faced with the decision to
change jobs and talked it over with several of my friends.
Imagine having the same conversation about five times.
Each time you're saying the same thing somehow hoping
that you will receive the answer you're looking for or at
least an answer that will help you feel good about the
decision that you have made. Perhaps I'm the only person
who has done this, but I now believe that I was talking to
all of my friends about it because I was not at peace with
the decision I made. I needed clarity and I was seeking it in
the wrong place.

Many times in life, we choose to talk about our issues and
decisions with everyone except God. By the time we take
the problem to Him, we are hearing so many voices and are
so distracted that we cannot hear God's voice or the
direction He is leading us in. Today's verse says that our
own ears will **hear** His voice and He will tell us which way
to go.

I have since learned to seek God's guidance first. There have been times where I've been tempted to step outside of God's will in a rush to get a quick answer but the Holy Spirit gently reminds me that God is waiting to hear from me to provide direction.

Keep your mind and heart clear of all the other voices by seeking God through prayer and His word. Should there be someone you need to discuss your situation with, He will reveal that too! Remember to seek godly counsel!

Today I encourage you to filter out the other voices so that you can hear what God is instructing you to do.

Prayer for Today: Father, in the name of Jesus, please give me wisdom to seek you first in all things. Give me guidance and direction like never before. I pray that you let your voice be so clear to me that I will be certain that it is you speaking to me. I only want to do your will. In Jesus' name I pray, Amen.

For further study, read Matthew 6:33 and Isaiah 30 in its entirety.

DAY 12

JOURNAL

Life Questions/Application

1. What issues have I been talking to everyone about but God? Take a moment now and take them to the Lord in prayer.

2. Have I been asking people and not God to give me guidance regarding my purpose? Lord please clear my mind and heart so that I may clearly hear your instructions.

3. What distractions in my life prevent me from hearing God's voice?

DAY 13 - Who's Going With Me?

Exodus 33:15-16 NLT
Then Moses said, "If you don't personally go with us, don't make us leave this place. 16 How will anyone know that you look favorably on me—on me and on your people—if you don't go with us? For your presence among us sets your people and me apart from all other people on the earth."

In this passage, and throughout the book of Exodus, Moses is leading the Israelites into the Promised Land. The Lord has chosen and spoken to Moses to lead His people. The Lord gave Moses a series of tasks to complete on His behalf in front of the Israelites in order that they may believe that the Lord sent Moses. Moses spent much time with the Lord praying, communicating and worshiping Him. Still, Moses needed more to accomplish his task. Moses needed God's glory! He needed God to not just give him instructions but to go with him! He knew that if the task God wanted Him to complete was to be completed, God needed to go with him. Everyone else needed to know and see that God was with him too.

Today as you contemplate what's before you, think about who is with you. Think about who gave you the instructions. Are you following the instructions? Did you ask the Lord to go with you?

Sometimes when you share your dreams, goals, or purpose with others, you will not get the response you're expecting. You may not receive an offer to help or congratulatory remarks. However, remember that your purpose comes from God. You don't have to look to man to validate it. You cannot let others' opinions "put out your fire" or cause you to be any less excited about your dreams and what you have been called to do! God is with you!

Let your daily prayer mirror Moses' words to the Lord in our key verse. Remember that God's presence sets you apart from everyone else!

Prayer for Today: Lord God, I honor you and give your name all of the Praise! O most worthy God, let your presence fill me today. Go with me on the path that you have chosen for me. Lord, I ask that you forgive me of my sins and my moments of doubt and hesitation. I have faith in you and your will for my life. Give me courage to be bold and step out on faith to do what you have called me to do. I love you and thank you for loving me in a way that only you can! In Jesus' name, Amen.

For further study, read the entire chapter of Exodus 33 and Proverbs 3:5-6.

DAY 13

JOURNAL

Life Questions/Application

1. Have I asked the Lord to let His presence rest and abide within me so that I may accomplish the task(s) that He has given me? Why or why not?

2. Am I seeking validation from others in regard to the assignment that GOD has given me? Am I afraid? Am I sure of what GOD has called me to do at this time in my life? What can I do so that I will be sure?

3. Have I been spending quality time reading and studying God's word? Am I giving God enough of my time so that I may hear His voice? How can I be sure of this?

DAY 14 - LOOK STRAIGHT AHEAD

Proverbs 4:25-27 NLT
Look straight ahead, and fix your eyes on what lies before you. Mark out a straight path for your feet; stay on the safe path. Don't get sidetracked; keep your feet from following evil.

When God gives you an assignment, you have to stay focused. Once you purpose in your heart to follow God's instructions, there will be many distractions to come up against you in an attempt to get you off course.

The scripture says to fix your eyes on what lies before you. Think about the driver who turns his head to the left or right to stare at a sign. The car will drift toward the direction in which the driver is looking causing the driver to be in the wrong lane. The same thing happens in your life each day. Your life will head in the direction that your heart and mind are focused upon. If you are not careful, you will end up in the wrong lane as well.

The scripture also says to "mark out a straight path for your feet." Get organized! When you have a written plan, the more likely you are to accomplish your goals. Your written plan will serve as a constant reminder of where you should be directing your energy.

Today, I encourage you to think about what you are focused on. Make sure you have a written plan to reference that mirrors God's plan for you.

There will ALWAYS be situations and people that will try to get you to lose focus and fix your eyes on anything and everything that is not leading you towards your goal. Satan's objective is to keep you from accomplishing yours!

This is why it is so important to know where you are going and have a written plan; otherwise you will waver and proceed in a different direction every time there is uncertainty or an obstacle. When you're living on purpose and encounter a distraction, you'll be able to identify it as such and know that its purpose is to keep you from accomplishing your mission. You will be able to dismiss the distraction and keep moving forward with what you have been called out to do.

Prayer for Today: Lord God, I come to you with praise on my lips. Hallelujah to your name, O God! Your name alone is worthy to be praised. In the name of Jesus, please forgive me of my sins as I forgive others through your power. Give me a steadfast heart. Speak to me about the plans you have for my life and how I may continue to glorify you! My goal is to give you glory in every area of my life. I bind distractions in the name of Jesus! Help me identify distractions. Thank you for bringing me back to you all of the times I've fallen. I honor you and thank you just for being who you are. I thank you for your power and presence in my life. In Jesus' name, Amen.

For further study, please read James 1:2-8, Psalm 23 (emphasis on v. 3) and Psalm 25:9.

DAY 14

JOURNAL

Life Questions/Applications

1. What are the distractions in my life that often get me sidetracked from accomplishing my God given tasks?

2. What can I do today that will help me eliminate these distractions so that I may hear God's voice clearly and stay on track with what He has called me to do?

3. Keep a separate journal for three days to document life after distractions are eliminated. How much more time do I have to spend with God? What is He saying to me?

DAY 15 - FOUNDATION OF WISDOM

Proverbs 9:10 NLT
Fear of the Lord is the foundation of wisdom. Knowledge of the Holy One results in good judgment.

What happens when you fear the Lord? The word of God tells us that fear is the foundation of wisdom. Fearing God is having a reverence for Him and acknowledging who He is in all of His power. Fearing God is knowing what He is capable of, grasping His sovereignty and knowing that it is He who made you. You belong to him; everything on this Earth belongs to him (Psalms 24:1) and He can do whatever He pleases. It is also knowing that you absolutely need Him every day. It is knowing that, without Him, you can do nothing, but all things are possible with Him.

I believe that when you really fear the Lord, you began to think differently. You recognize that the Lord is Holy and that you must praise and worship Him. You walk in the knowledge that you must praise Him with your whole being. You began to rely on him for everything. You think about the consequences of your actions before you act to make sure your ways are pleasing to God.

I believe that when you really fear the Lord, you began to act differently. You are a living representation of Christ. Your actions are an outward manifestation of what you think and what is in your heart. You change the way that you talk because you don't want to bring shame to the name of the Lord. You change the places you go, the company you keep and many of the things you do.

Fearing the Lord (really knowing who He is in all of His power) causes you to think and act differently and therefore produces wisdom. When you think and act differently, you walk in wisdom and knowledge, therefore becoming the person who God has predestined you to be.

Prayer for Today: Father God, I come to you today with reverence for your Holy name. I seek to please you with everything that's within me. I ask that you forgive me of my sins and cleanse me of everything that is not like you. Let me find comfort in your power and presence. Teach me about who you are that I may fear you and have wisdom. In order to fear you, I must know you in all of your glory! Your Word says that as I draw near to you, you will draw near to me. Draw near to me so that I may develop knowledge and wisdom. In Jesus' name, Amen.

For further study, please read Romans 12:2 and Romans 12:12-14.

DAY 15

JOURNAL

Life Questions/Application

1. Before I speak and act, do I consider my relationship with the Lord and how my actions and words may affect others? Why or why not? What can I do daily that will cause me to be more mindful of my ways so that I can bring glory to God's name?

2. Am I walking in wisdom? How do I know? How can I assure myself that I am walking in wisdom and learning God's will for my life?

DAY 16 – Becoming Future Focused

Isaiah 43:18 NLT
Forget the former things; do not dwell on the past.

Just the other day while getting ready for work, the Holy Spirit began to speak to me about my future. I believe that the Lord needed to get my attention because my past started to creep up on me. I began to think about some mistakes that I've made or things that I should have done. Thinking about those things casted a slight shadow of doubt about current projects that I am working on and caused me to wonder if I could really get to my pre-ordained destiny. In that instant, I was reminded of a sermon that I heard last year. Luckily for me, I had it on CD, so I listened to it on my way to work that morning.

The title of the sermon is "A Conversation About the Future." I listened to the sermon and everything the pastor said in the message resonated in my Spirit. That was exactly what I needed to hear in that moment. One statement that constantly rings in my mind is: "Don't let what you have not done, stop you from what you can do." In other words, do not allow your past limit you. Do not give your past any power over your future! Do not become weary or disheartened; God knows what your resume looks like. He did not choose you in error; He chose you because there is something within you that He wants to utilize to help someone else.

Many times when we think about our past, we can become consumed with it. When we become consumed, all we're thinking or even talking about is what we did or did not do last month, last year or even 5 years ago. (Remember that thoughts manifest into actions, and in this case, our speech). When we're constantly referencing and thinking about our past, we can't possibly be focused on our future.

I urge you to stop dwelling on the past. Instead concentrate on your incredible future. The question now becomes, "Will you accept your calling and move forward?" You can do all things through Christ who is your strength **(See Philippians 4:13).** Please know that the enemy wants you to focus on your past because that means you are not focused on your future. You are not moving forward. The enemy doesn't want you to seek God; he wants you to be stuck in the former things. He wants you to be preoccupied with anything that will keep you away from your destiny.

In verse 19, the Lord is saying that He is going to do a "new thing." Isn't that exciting? The "new thing" may very well be something out of your comfort zone! Allow the Holy Spirit to move in your life! Learn from the old, let go of the past and seek God for the "new" that He is going to do in you and through you.

Prayer for Today: Father God, thank you for the destiny that you've created just for me through you. Shield my mind that I may focus on what's ahead of me and not dwell on what has already happened. Help me to learn from the past and to keep my mind focused on moving forward in what you have in store for me. In Jesus' name, Amen.

For further study, please read Isaiah 43 in its entirety and Philippians 3:12-14.

DAY 16

JOURNAL

Life Questions/Application

1. Have I been focusing on something that has happened in the past instead of what God is currently calling me to do? Why does it keep resurfacing in my heart and mind? What can I do today to move past it and focus on what God is calling me to do?

2. What should I be focused on? What can I do to consistently focus on this?

DAY 17 - BE STEADFAST

Isaiah 7:9b NLT
Unless your faith is firm, I cannot make you stand firm.

Have you ever set your heart and mind out to accomplish a specific task and the very next thing you know, obstacle after obstacle appears in your life? A family member gets sick, unplanned expense puts your finances in a bind? Have you shared your vision or goal with someone else and they unknowingly speak death to your idea? Do the faithless naysayers have you worried about the things that *have* or might happen in an attempt to get you off track? Are you now concerned about whether or not you are on the right path? You have just shifted from a spirit of excitement to worry.

Worrying is an attack of the enemy. If you spend your time worrying about what might happen, you're distracted. You're not focused on your assignment. Worrying never has and never will change anything. Consider Jesus' words in Matthew 6:34 NLT, *"So don't worry about tomorrow, for tomorrow will bring its own worries. Today's trouble is enough for today."*

As I read our scripture text today, the Holy Spirit reminded me to stand firm in the faith and to remain unmovable and unfazed by the things that are going on around me. The Holy Spirit also reminded me not to worry about things that might or could happen. My job is to complete the assignment given to me. It is often easy to start something and harder to finish it. Earlier in the chapter, King Ahaz received word that Jerusalem was about to be attacked. This caused him to tremble with fear. Later on in the chapter, the Lord sent Isaiah to King Ahaz to tell him to stop worrying and confirmed to him what *will* happen.

Even though plans were made to attack Jerusalem, they were not carried out. Remember that the Lord has the ultimate power and nothing can happen unless He allows it. So instead of focusing on life's issues, concentrate on God and your assignment. No matter what happens, God's plan and purpose for your life will prevail. Ponder Job's statement in Job 42:2 which says, *"I know that you can do all things; no purpose of yours can be thwarted."*

Today I want to encourage you to ignore the negative voices. Keep doing God's perfect will by allowing the Holy Spirit guide you. Be firm! Be steadfast! Keep the faith! God will surely make you stand firm (give you success) when your faith is firm!

Prayer for Today: Father God, as always, your Word is very timely. It is a reminder of your care for me. Thank you for being all knowing and sovereign. Thank you for your goodness and kindness. As I lift up your name right now, I take comfort in knowing that you care for me and that you know exactly what I need. Thank you for reminding me of who you are and what you have called me to do! I give you glory and praise! Thank you for loving me in spite of my sin. Please forgive me of my sins and help me to become more like you while completing the assignments that you've given me. In Jesus' name, Amen.

For further study, please read Matthew 6:25-34 and Isaiah 7 in its entirety.

DAY 17

JOURNAL

Life Questions/Application

1. What or who are the negative voices in my life that are causing me to worry and not complete my assignment? What can I do to remove the negativity?

2. Am I allowing the Holy Spirit to lead me or the negativity? If the Holy Spirit is not leading me, how can I get back on the right pathway?

DAY 18 - God With Us

Isaiah 7:14 NLT
All right then, the Lord himself will give you the sign. Look! The virgin will conceive a child! She will give birth to a son and will call him Immanuel (which means 'God is with us').

Several years ago (nearly five years), Pastor Benford, The Living Word Fellowship Church, preached a sermon titled "With Me Is God." Throughout the message he used our scripture text as a reference. He explained that Immanuel meant "God with us." However, he urged us to look at it this way: "With Me Is God." Now I must be honest. I don't remember many sermons (especially without studying them repeatedly) but this one has stayed with me since the morning I heard it. I can still hear his final words: "If y'all don't remember anything else, remember this: With Me Is God."

Immanuel is one of the many names of God! I know that we each experience moments in our lives when we pause to wonder if God is there and if He's listening to our prayers. Take comfort in knowing that He is there and He does hear your prayers. His name describes who He is! He is with you! He will never leave you nor forsake you. He is omnipresent!!

So today I want to pass this on to you: if you must remind yourself daily, then please do. It helps and it is surely comforting and empowering to know that "With Me Is God." Never lose sight of it. In order to fully appreciate this fact, we must know the **power** of God's presence and what it means to actually have His presence in our lives each day. I pray that you come to know, understand, appreciate and experience the power of God's presence in your life.

***Prayer for Today*:** In the name of Jesus, Lord I come to you right now thanking you for your power and your presence in my life. Help me to see and recognize you at work in my life daily. Forgive me for not acknowledging your presence. Forgive me of the sins I've committed against you. Lord thank you for never leaving me nor forsaking me. Thank you for being with me wherever I go. In Jesus' name, Amen.

For further study, please read Joshua 1 in its entirety and Psalm 25:9.

DAY 18

JOURNAL

Life Questions/Application

1. Am I concerned that God is not with me or that I am not hearing His voice? If so, what can I do to be sure of God's presence in my life?

2. Am I spending enough time with God praying and studying? How is this manifested in my life?

DAY 19 - Giving God the Glory

Isaiah 26:12 NLT
Lord, you will grant us peace; all we have accomplished is really from you.

What does it mean to give God glory? After reading and meditating on a few scriptures, I am convinced that we give glory to God when we praise Him, thank Him and acknowledge Him for *who* He is and for all that He has done.

During my sophomore year in high school, I took a driver's education course. Whenever we would practice driving, there would always be one student driver, the instructor and three student passengers. One day when it was my turn to drive, we took a trip downtown. The only available parking was parallel parking spaces. I absolutely had no idea how to parallel park! I don't even think I knew what parallel parking was until that day! The instructor attempted to give me directions on how to maneuver the car into the parking space but I was still nervous, hesitant and clueless! Now for one thing, the car was a blue, huge "box Chevy." At the time, I was 5'1" and could hardly see over the steering wheel! I was pretty uncomfortable! To the best of my limited ability, I attempted to parallel park the car and all of a sudden the instructor reached over and took control of the steering wheel!

All I could feel was the steering wheel slipping beneath my sweaty palms as he maneuvered the car into the parking space. The most work I did was tapping the accelerator and brakes as instructed. Once we were finally parked, he looked over at me and said, "You didn't do that, I did that." Then he let out a soft chuckle.

I want to remind you today that "You didn't do that, God did that." The success and promotion on your job or in your career; the elevation in your finances and in your relationships, God did it! Even the things that are taken for granted: sight, touch, taste, hearing and activity of limbs are all gifts from God! Acknowledge the Lord by remembering Him and honoring Him for everything BIG and small in your life. You are where you are today because of the Lord's power, His blessings, His favor, His graciousness, His mercy and grace.

You must give glory to God because He did it for you and through you. Never take God's glory and praise because you did not accomplish anything on your own. It is all a gift from Him. Remember that the works that God perform through you and for you are for *His* glory!

Prayer for Today: Father God, I give your name honor and glory because you deserve it. Please forgive me for any time that I may not have acknowledged your presence or work in my life. Thank you for all that you've done for me and through me. I thank you even more for what's to come. Help me to always be mindful of your power and presence in my life. In Jesus' name, you're worthy, Amen!

For further study, please read Psalm 44:8; Psalm 86:12, and Jeremiah 13:16.

DAY 19

JOURNAL

Life Questions/Application

1. Has there been a recent moment in my life where I've taken the credit when the credit belonged to God? What happened?

2. What is God currently doing in my life? What can I do now to make sure He gets the glory both now and later?

DAY 20 - Fulfilling the Requirements

Luke 12:48 NLT
But someone who does not know, and then does something wrong, will be punished only lightly. When someone has been given much, much will be required in return; and when someone has been entrusted with much, even more will be required.

Have you ever been at a place in your life where God has constantly blessed you to achieve success after success? Or, have you ever been in the opposite place? A place where you've felt like you've worked and worked but have not yet experienced the reward of your hard work?

Have you found yourself longing for the moment where you can take a break, but at the same time you have so much that you need and want to accomplish?

One day as I was driving home from work, the Holy Spirit spoke to me with the key verse. There may come a time in your life where the temptation comes to want to slow down and "chill." The reason you aren't "chilling" is because you are destined for greatness! God has chosen you to carry out His will! God has placed so much in you that He needs to get out of you. You may find yourself wanting to take a short cut at work, in your personal life, in your spiritual life or even trying to get to your destiny. Remember, God requires so much more of you. He requires that you give your very best.

In order to determine what is required of you, I think you need to know what it is you're trying to accomplish and why you want to accomplish it. For example, think of two students matriculating through college who are studying two different programs. Lets say one student is a chemical engineering major while the other is an English major. The courses that are required of each student are different and each student must meet the requirements of their own respective programs in order to earn their degrees. Now, the English major may enroll in a course that was designed for the chemical engineering major and vice versa, but success in the course does not help him fulfill the requirements to complete his program. Although everything is permissible, not all things are beneficial. **See 1 Corinthians 10:23.**

Everyone is not on the same "degree plan" as you are in life so resist the temptation to do the same thing your neighbor is doing. Your neighbor may not "prepare like you" because your neighbor may not be required to do so. Your neighbor is not trying to accomplish the same thing you're trying to accomplish. Therefore, know what God requires of you in everything that you set out to do.

We are required to do everything as if we are doing it to the Lord **(See Colossians 3:23).** We do not all have the same assignment. When you know your assignment, you'll know what's required of you. If your spirit is overflowing with vision and dreams, God expects you to give your best as you work to turn them into reality.

Prayer for Today: Father in Heaven, thank you for all you have done for me. Thank you for the purpose that you've given me. Give me wisdom and knowledge to know and do what is required of me so that I may please you. Help me to resist the urge to do what my neighbor is doing. Instead, help me honor you while doing what is required of me. In Jesus' name, Amen.

For further study, please read Micah 6:8, Genesis 26:4-6 and Deuteronomy 10:11-13.

DAY 20

JOURNAL

Life Questions/Application

1. What does God require of me to fulfill my assignment? Am I doing all that is required?

2. What can I do to make sure that I remain purposeful?

3. What are some other assignments that I'm working on? Could these extra assignments be draining me? Are they interfering with what God has called me to do? What assignments can be put on hold or given less time?

DAY 21 - No Compromise

Daniel 3:28 NLT
Then Nebuchadnezzar said, "Praise to the God of Shadrach, Meshach, and Abednego! He sent his angel to rescue his servants who trusted in him. They defied the king's command and were willing to die rather than serve or worship any god except their own God.

How do you handle tough situations? Do you handle them in the same manner as Shadrach, Meshach and Abednego? In this chapter, King Nebuchadnezzar created a gold statue and ordered everyone to bow down and worship it at the sound of the instruments. In this familiar passage, Shadrach, Meshach and Abednego refused to bow down and worship any god besides the Most High God. They were thrown into a fiery furnace that was heated seven times its normal temperature because of the king's fury with their disobedience to his decree. We learn that the heat of the furnace was no comparison to God's power. We also know that it was really hot because the soldiers who threw them into the fire were killed by flames. Once the king saw the three of them and whom I believe was God walking around inside the furnace, unbound and unharmed, the king ordered them out and noticed that they were not burned. Their hair didn't even smell of smoke. Most importantly, King Nebuchadnezzar acknowledged that God is the Most High God and that no god can rescue like Him. The king became a believer because of the obedience of those three men!

I'd like to pull from this passage and encourage you today. First, remain faithful to God regardless of your circumstances. God's power is much greater than anyone's power here on earth and in the heavens. After all, he is the giver of power. Secondly, remember that even if you do find yourself in a "hot" situation, God is faithful and just enough to save and deliver (rescue) you. Once you remain faithful and acknowledge God in all you do, you will be promoted! That situation of oppression will become an opportunity!

In our scripture passage, God used the king in that, he being the very person who tried to kill them, as the same person who promoted them. Your elevation will come from your faithfulness. We also learn that we do not mistreat others throughout the heat of unpleasant situations. Continue to walk in destiny regardless of your present circumstances. Your obedience will also encourage those around you. Remember that there are times that you are chosen to go through difficult situations because the Lord trusts you enough to respond well. When you do respond in a manner pleasing to God, you will help draw those around you closer to Him.

Prayer for Today: Oh Most Holy and Gracious God, I come into your presence with praise! I declare that you are God alone and I worship you with everything that is within me! Thank you for being faithful. Thank you for your loving kindness and your mercy. Help me to remain steadfast and faithful to you regardless of my circumstance. In Jesus' name, Amen.

For further study, please read Psalm 84:11 and Daniel 3 in its entirety.

DAY 21

JOURNAL

Life Questions/Application

1. On my path to destiny, have I compromised what I believe in order that I may please others? What did I do and why? What can I do to remain unwavering in my faith?

2. What current circumstances can I exercise my faith and trust in God to do all that He promised?

DAY 22 - There is Still Time

Jeremiah 18:6-10 NLT

"O Israel, can I not do to you as this potter has done to his clay? As the clay is in the potter's hand, so are you in my hand. If I announce that a certain nation or kingdom is to be uprooted, torn down, and destroyed, but then that nation renounces its evil ways, I will not destroy it as I had planned. And if I announce that I will plant and build up a certain nation or kingdom, but then that nation turns to evil and refuses to obey me, I will not bless it as I said I would.

In the previous chapters of the Book of Jeremiah, the Lord repeatedly speaks about destroying His people for constantly disobeying Him, ignoring Him and worshiping idols. Verse 8 states that if his people would turn from their evil ways and follow Him, He would not destroy them as planned. He also says that He will build up a nation and if the nation turns away from Him, and disobeys, He will no longer bless them.

Consider whether or not you are on the right path. If you are, continue on the right path and do not give in to the temptations of this world. There are so many sins to get entangled in and cause you to lose focus and get sidetracked. Remember, your goal is to complete your assignments and walk in destiny. Remember, the enemy's goal is just the opposite--to keep you from completing your assignments and walking in destiny.

If you are not on the right path, there is still time to get on the right track. It is never too late to do what you have been called to do. It is your calling! It is your destiny! If you turn around and follow God, he will bless you and lead you. God is faithful, merciful and kind. He welcomes His children back to Him. Seek Him with your whole heart today and get back to walking in destiny.

One may ask the question, how do I get on the right path? Consider how you got off the path chosen for you. Retrace your steps. Do the opposite of what you've been doing. Repent to the Lord and turn away from the things that do not please God. Ask God for direction and spend time in His word. God answers prayers so continue to seek Him. He will certainly show you the way that you should go.

Prayer for Today: Lord God I love you because you first loved me. Thank you for caring about every detail of my life. Thank you that you have plans for me and want me to reach my destiny. Thank you for your patience. Thank you for keeping me on the right path and accepting me back when I turned from you. You're more awesome than I can ever imagine. Thank you for your goodness, In Jesus' name, Amen.

For further study, please read Jeremiah 18, Proverbs 3:5-8 and Galatians 1:15-16.

DAY 22

JOURNAL

Life Questions/Application

1. Am I on the path that God has chosen for me? How do I know?

2. What can I do to stay on track?

3. What are some things that have caused me to get off track? What can I do to not allow these things to get me off track in the future?

DAY 23 - No Doubt

Isaiah 1:2-3 NLT
Listen, O heavens! Pay attention, earth! This is what the Lord says: "The children I raised and cared for have rebelled against me. Even an ox knows its owner, and a donkey recognizes its master's care—but Israel doesn't know its master. My people don't recognize my care for them."

I posted a scripture along with encouraging words on a social networking site. A family member sent me a private message, thanked me for the encouraging words and said she needed to hear them. In response I said, "No problem. Remember that God loves you. Be encouraged." She further responded by saying that I was acting like she doesn't go to church. She knows that God loves her. Her statement resonated with me. As I pondered her statement, it bothered me; it left me unsettled.

Is it enough to attend church services weekly? Are we listening to the messages? Why are we such broken people? Why are we still hurting and allowing others to hurt us? Why are we not growing like we should? Do we know what it really means to have God's love? Do we really understand the power of God's love? Do we really believe in the power of God's love? Do we believe God's love can heal us? Save us? Deliver us? Sustain us? Encourage us? Is God's love always with us?

I could continue with the questions but as I began reading this chapter, God answered the questions on my heart with today's key verse. The truth is that many of God's people do not truly know God and therefore do not know His love.

I urge you to make room for time with the Lord in your daily life. Make time in His presence a priority. When you spend time in His presence praying, worshiping, praising and studying His word, you learn more about Him and His love for you. He also reveals His plans for you and gives you direction when you spend time in His presence.

Prayer for Today: Father God, today I praise you and honor your name just for being who you are in all of your greatness. I ask forgiveness for the moments where I had the time to spend with you but I chose to do something else. I ask that you show me areas in my life where I can eliminate activities and use that time to spend with you and get to know you more. Thank you for your patience and kindness. Thank you for your grace and mercy. In Jesus' name, Amen.

> **For further study, please read Isaiah 1, Ephesians 2 and Ephesians 3:18-19.**

DAY 23

JOURNAL

Life Questions/Application

1. What causes me to doubt God's love for me?

2. Have I made spending time with the Lord a priority? Why or why not? How do I know? What can I do to be consistent with spending time in God's presence?

DAY 24 - Learning From the Ants

Proverbs 6:6-8 NLT
Take a lesson from the ants, you lazybones. Learn from their ways and become wise! Though they have no prince or governor or ruler to make them work, they labor hard all summer, gathering food for the winter.

Ants work really hard don't they? As a child, I can remember peering down at two long, long lines of ants carrying food. I could actually see small pieces of food (possibly bread) on their backs. One line was leaving the ant colony and the other line (carrying food) was heading back to the colony. There are several things that we can learn from ants.

First, ants have a preparation and planning spirit. They work in the summer, gathering food for the winter. That means they begin preparing for the winter two seasons before winter even occurs. I did some quick research on ants. Did you know that carpenter ants gather food to feed the next generation? When the first generation of worker ants mature, they work to increase the food supply for the colony. Colonies can consist of thousands and thousands of ants. One can learn a lot from the ants here. Always plan ahead and prepare for your next step. You have to be prepared when your opportunity presents itself. I believe that sometimes your opportunities are waiting on *you* to get ready.

Secondly, the ants do not need to be micromanaged. They don't need someone to rule or watch over them to make sure the task is getting accomplished. (v.7) Likewise, when you're at work each day, take initiative. Many of us already know what needs to be done day to day and do not need to be micromanaged. In relation to planning, make a list of the tasks that need to be completed for each day. "Own your work." When you take initiative, see projects through to the end and do more than what's expected, advancement and success are inevitable.

Lastly, ants do not work alone. When you see one ant, it is always traveling with other ants that share the same mission! You should have someone helping you accomplish your goals who can work along with you. Working with someone who has already accomplished what you're trying to accomplish is even better. It is important to have a support system. Consider **Ecclesiastes 4:9-10** which tells us, *"Two are better than one, because they have a good return for their labor: If either of them falls down, one can help the other up. But pity anyone who falls and has no one to help them up."*

I also want to encourage you to surround yourself with other people who have goals. If not, you just may find yourself being sidetracked or being a "lazybone"—not accomplishing anything. 1 Corinthians 15:33 says *"Do not be misled: Bad company corrupts good character."*

Prayer for Today: Dear Lord, I come to you today with my heart overflowing with thanksgiving and praise! Thank you for your new mercies today! Please search my heart and forgive me of my sins and unrighteousness. Help me to be a person who plans, works hard and works well with others to accomplish the purpose for which you have created me. Give me wisdom and knowledge. I can't do anything without you and I want you to know that I need you now and forever. In Jesus' name, Amen.

For further study, please read Ecclesiastes 4:9-12, Psalm 33:10-12 and Psalm 40:4-6.

DAY 24

JOURNAL

Life Questions/Application

1. What have I done to prepare and plan for the assignment that God has given me?

2. Have I taken ownership of this assignment?
   a. I have taken ownership by

   b. I have not taken ownership of my assignment because

3. Who is my mentor? Who is assisting me in completing my God given assignment in this season of my life?

DAY 25 - PLEASANT THOUGHTS

PSALM 104:34 NLT
May all my thoughts be pleasing to him, for I rejoice in the Lord.

As a Christian, you should desire to have thoughts that please God. You should desire to live your life in such a way that it honors God. You should also desire to become more like Christ each and every day.

To become more like Christ, your thoughts must first be pleasing to Him. You have to change the way you think. The things you meditate on determine the direction of your life.

How do you get to the point where you have pleasing thoughts? The first thing you must do is be careful about what you fix your eyes upon. *Psalm 101:3 NLT states "I will refuse to look at anything vile and vulgar."* The NKJV states, *"I will set no wicked thing before my eyes."* What are you watching on TV or the internet? What are you reading? Think about it. How many times have you saw something, thought about it, then went to get it? What you see drives your thoughts and your thoughts drive your actions.

The second thing you must do is be careful about what you listen to. *James 1:21 NLT says "So get rid of all the filth and evil in your lives, and humbly accept the word God has planted in your hearts, for it has the power to save your souls."* What do you listen to on the radio? What people are you listening to? What are these people saying? God's word cannot be planted in your heart unless you actively listen to it. It will benefit you to pay attention to what the pastor is saying when you're at church.

James 1:22 says "But don't just listen to God's word. You must do what it says. Otherwise, you are only fooling yourselves."

The last thing you must do to have thoughts pleasing to God is train your thoughts. You cannot get to this place over night. You must continue to work at it and be intentional. *Philippians 4:8b NLT says "Fix your thoughts on what is true, and honorable, and right and pure, and lovely, and admirable. Think about things that are excellent and worthy of praise."*

I encourage you to ask God to give you the desire (if you don't already have it) to have pleasing thoughts. Make a conscious effort to guard your eyes and ears from things that are not pleasing to God and that will take you in the opposite direction of where God wants you to go. Lastly, train your thoughts. Make a conscious effort each day to meditate on those things in which Philippians 4:8 instructs you to meditate.

Prayer for Today: Father in the name of Jesus, I come to you with a heart that is eager to please you. I lift up your name today O God! Hallelujah to your name because you deserve the highest praise! Give me the desire to have thoughts that please you. Help me to be mindful of what I watch and who and what I listen to. Give me the craving to meditate on those things which please you. In Jesus' name, Amen.

For further study, please read Luke 11:34-36 and James 1 in its entirety.

DAY 25

JOURNAL

Life Questions/Application

1. What do I spend my time watching? What do I spend my time listening to? Who do I spend my time talking to? What do I spend my time reading?

2. Are these things drawing me closer to God or pulling me away? What things should I eliminate and replace so that I may walk closer with my Lord and Savior?

DAY 26 – The Righteous are Remembered

Psalm 112:5-6 NLT
Good comes to those who lend money generously and conduct their business fairly. Such people will not be overcome by evil. Those who are righteous will be long remembered.

Have you ever worked at a company where lying, cheating and manipulating others to get ahead was rampant? Perhaps you're working at a place like that right now. Rest assured that you don't have to do any of those things to progress in your career or fulfill your purpose.

One of the most difficult places to live out our faith consistently is probably the workplace. That's where most of us spend our time at least five days per week. That is probably where we experience the most hell: gossiping, backbiting, adultery, jealously, lying and the like. However, we must rise above all of these things and daily put on the whole armor of God **(Ephesians 6:13-17)** to keep from stumbling into one of satan's subtle traps. You should not allow the behavior of others to corrupt your character. Whether you like it or not, you are being examined. Your actions (and not just what you say) will either help or hinder your neighbor. Therefore, let your light shine! Your faithfulness has the power to inspire those around you to live right as well.

No matter where you spend your time each day, you are always being watched because you bear the name of Christ as Christian. Others are watching to see how you handle life's ups and downs. Your attitude and behavior should positively affect others. You should live your life in such a way that glorifies God and inspires others to do the same.

Today I want to encourage you to diligently seek and remain faithful to God. Love people. Be honest in your work. Be trustworthy. When you live this way, evil will not overcome you. As a matter of fact, "Surely goodness and mercy will follow you all the days of your life." **Psalm 23:6a**.

***Prayer for Today*:** Most Holy and Perfect God, Lord I come to you today with a heart full of thanksgiving, praise and reverence for your name. Thank you for being who you are. Thank you for your unfailing love and mercy. Thank you for being faithful even when I am unfaithful. Thank you for being unchanging. Lord I open my heart to you right now, asking that you purify me and give me the right spirit. I ask that you examine me and remove everything that's not like you. Teach me to live righteously. In your word, you told me that I would be long remembered if I did so. I believe that I will not be looked over but I will receive the best from you for my life. I honor you and praise you. I thank you for your goodness and mercy! In Jesus' name, Amen.

For further study, please read Deuteronomy 6 and Ephesians 6: 10-20.

DAY 26

JOURNAL

Life Questions/Applications

1. In order to accomplish my God-given tasks, am I treating others poorly? Am I trusting in God (no matter how long it's taking) to present preordained opportunities to move me forward into destiny?

2. Am I allowing the negative behavior of those around me to impact my behavior? If I am, what can I do to change so that I can be a positive influence?

DAY 27 - Joy In Obedience

Psalm 112:1
Praise the Lord! How joyful are those who fear the Lord and delight in obeying his commands.

Think about a time when you were faced with a difficult choice and you made the right decision—one pleasing to God? Didn't that bring joy and peace to your heart? How did it feel to reap the benefits of being faithful? Today's key verse says those who delight in obeying God's commands are joyful people. (Now if you've never made the right decision, today is a great day to start! God is forgiving!)

Now think about a time when you made the difficult choice not to follow God but to sin and do things your own way? Didn't that feel terrible? (Even if it did feel good in the beginning) Were you faced with "should haves, could haves and would haves?" Didn't that road lead to destruction? (More problems than you started with)

As you are faced with day to day decisions, remember the joy of following God and paying attention to His voice. Remember the peace you experienced and the joy of reaping God's abundant blessings. Listen to that still, small voice that steers you in the right direction. Seek God with your whole heart. Commit yourself to his will for EVERY area of your life. Your obedience stores up blessings for your children as well. *Psalm 112:2 states, "Their children will be blessed."* I am certain that you want the best for your children, so continue to walk in the path that God has set before you. Also know that even if you do not have children, your obedience or disobedience affects those connected to you. This indicates that someone connected to you will be blessed because of your faithfulness or miss out on blessings when you are unfaithful.

Your Creator knows what is best for you. Trust in Him.

***Prayer for Today*:** Father in Heaven, I love you and I honor you. I give your name praise because you are worthy. There is no one in heaven or on earth like you. I truly desire to please you so I ask now in Jesus' name that you forgive me of my sins. Help me to turn away from every unpleasing thing in your sight. I need your strength Lord. I want to make decisions that please you. I trust in you and commit my mind, body and spirit to you today. In Jesus' name, Amen.

For further study, please read Isaiah 56:3-5 and Proverbs 21:3.

DAY 27

JOURNAL

Life Questions/Application

1. What decision(s) am I facing today? What are the alternatives? Which alternative pleases God? Which alternative pleases my flesh?

2. Which alternative moves me closer to where I'm trying to go (destiny)?

3. God is calling me to make the decision to

DAY 28 - BUILDERS

Psalm 127:1 NLT
Unless the Lord builds a house, the work of the builders is wasted. Unless the Lord protects a city, guarding it with sentries will do no good.

What are you building? A relationship? A career? Who or what are you trusting in for protection? Whatever you do in this life, seeking God should be a priority. If you do not acknowledge God in your affairs, you have no reason to expect His blessings.

When it comes to life building, the meditational scripture teaches two things:

1. In order for you to succeed in any task, the Lord must be your leader. If it isn't His plan, then He isn't the one leading you and your work is in vain. The greatest undertaking will fail if God doesn't crown it with success!

Consider what is being built in your life. What foundation is it being built upon? To determine if the Lord is the builder, ask yourself the following questions: What am I doing? Why am I doing it? Who told me to do it? Who will receive the Glory? How am I getting it done? If you're doing it for selfish gain, then the Lord won't receive glory. Therefore, He is not the builder.

2. In biblical times, guards stood at the city gates to protect the city's citizens. If the guards cannot protect the city without God's presence, you cannot properly manage your affairs without God's presence. If God is for you, who can be against

you? **(See Romans 8:31)** There is no power greater than God's power.

So today I want you to think about who or what you may be depending on to protect you. Is it some material thing? Or is it the Lord?

You need the Lord on your side. Whatever you do, make sure that it pleases him. Submit to God's will and allow him to be the builder and protector in your life.

Prayer for Today: Father in heaven, I honor you and give you praise today! I lift up your name because you are most worthy of my praise. I seek to please you with my life. I ask now that you forgive me of my sins. Examine me that I may see myself for who I am in you. Search me and remove everything within me that's not like you. Forgive me for the times I strayed away and have not allowed you to be the builder, protector and shield in my life. I turn to you again because I want you to be my builder. I want to rely on you to protect me and shield me from seen and unseen danger. I need you Lord. I do not want to waste time building anything in vain or relying on something or someone other than you for protection over my life. I need you. In Jesus' name, Amen.

For further study, please read Psalm 27, Psalm 119:105 and Hebrews 3:4

DAY 28

JOURNAL

Life Questions/Application

1. What am I "building?" Where is my focus? Why am I focused on this? Is this where the Lord is directing me to exert my energy?

2. Am I following God's blueprint? How do I know? God has confirmed his instructions to me by

DAY 29 - FINDING FAVOR

Proverbs 3:1-4 NLT

My child, never forget the things I have taught you. Store my commands in your heart. If you do this, you will live many years, and your life will be satisfying. Never let loyalty and kindness leave you! Tie them around your neck as a reminder. Write them deep within your heart. Then you will find favor with both God and people, and you will earn a good reputation.

What does it mean to find favor? What does favor mean? The dictionary defines favor as "something done or granted out of goodwill, rather than from justice or for remuneration; a kind act." It is also defined as "excessive kindness or unfair partiality; preferential treatment." Finding favor with God has been defined as gaining approval, acceptance, or special benefits or blessings. We all want favor with both God and those around us wherever we go. In the scripture reference above, Solomon gives instructions on what one must do to find favor.

In verse 1, he says to never forget the things he taught. If you refer to chapter 2, he continually instructs the reader to seek wisdom and knowledge. The entire chapter points out the benefits of having wisdom. Some of which are: *The Lord is a shield to those who walk with integrity; Wise choices will watch over you; Understanding will keep you safe; Wisdom will save you from evil people.* (verses 7b,11-12)

Next you must never let loyalty and kindness leave you. Consistently love others and remain faithful to the Lord. When you seek and receive wisdom, you will learn how to walk in love and faithfulness.

Keep this message before you. How? By constantly living it out each day. Each day, seek wisdom by studying and meditating on God's word. Allow the love of God within you to be evident in your daily actions. When you do these things, the bible promises that you will find favor with both God and man.

Prayer for Today: Father God, I give you praise, honor and glory! You are most worthy of my praise. Please be kind and merciful to me and forgive me of my sins as I forgive others. Create in me a clean heart and renew the right spirit within me. Lord I come to you seeking wisdom today. Proverbs 2:6 says that you grant wisdom and from your mouth comes knowledge and understanding. Please grant me this one request today. I know that if I have wisdom, I have abundant life. I thank you now! Oh Lord, I love you and praise you. In Jesus' name, Amen.

For further study, please read Proverbs 2 and Matthew 22:38-40.

DAY 29

JOURNAL

Life Questions/Application

1. Have I committed to spending time in God's word daily so that I can walk in the path that He has set before me?

2. God requires that I love my neighbors as I love myself. Am I kind to others as a reflection of my love for God and the purpose He has for my life? If not, what can I do today to commit to being the person God has called me to be?

DAY 30 - Obedience Reaps Blessings

Genesis 26:2-6 NIV
The Lord appeared to Isaac and said, "Do not go down to Egypt; live in the land where I tell you to live. Stay in this land for a while, and I will be with you and will bless you. For to you and your descendants I will give all these lands and will confirm the oath I swore to your father Abraham. I will make your descendants as numerous as the stars in the sky and will give them all these lands, and through your offspring all nations on earth will be blessed, because Abraham obeyed me and kept my requirements, my commands, my decrees and my laws," So Isaac stayed in Gerar.

We learn in Genesis 26 that obedience reaps blessings! The Lord told Isaac to stay put where he was. You see, in this particular chapter, there was a famine in the land: little food and water. But the Lord wanted to show Isaac his sovereignty and bless him right where He was. God promised him that if he trusted in Him and went where He told him to go, that He would bless him.

Isaac was obedient to what the Lord asked him to do. Given his current situation, I imagine that Isaac probably wondered to himself why the Lord would want Him to stay there when there was a famine in the land. Nevertheless, Isaac obeyed God. His obedience reaped blessings! Not only were God's promises manifested in his life because of his obedience but he received them in that *same year*.

Genesis 26: 12-13 NIV *Isaac planted crops in that land and the same year reaped a hundredfold, because the Lord blessed him. The man became rich, and his wealth continued to grow until he became very wealthy.*

Not only did God promise to bless him but He also promised to be with Isaac throughout it all.

Genesis 26:24 *That night the Lord appeared to him and said, "I am the Lord of your father Abraham. Do not be afraid, for I am with you; I will bless you and will increase the number of your descendants for the sake of my servant Abraham."*

No matter what you're facing in life today, be obedient to what God has already told you to do. Perhaps there's a "famine in your life" and you know exactly where to go or what to do to be sustained during this time. God has promised to bless you immeasurably and to never leave you. He can bless you right where you are!

***Prayer for Today*:** Lord God in the name of Jesus, I come to you thanking you for your sovereignty. I'm in a season of famine oh God and I need you right away. Help me to not walk outside of your will but be patient and wait on your direction. I need your blessings and presence more than anything because I know that no one can bless me like you can. In Jesus' name, Amen.

Read the entire chapter of Genesis 26 for further study.

DAY 30

JOURNAL

Life Question/Application

1. Am I experiencing a "famine like" situation in my life today? I know where I can go to solve the problem(s) immediately but God wants me to be patient where I am. I must trust God and do what He has called me to do. God has called me to

THE INVITATION

John 3:16 NLT
For God loved the world so much that he gave his one and only Son, so that everyone who believes in him will not perish but have eternal life.

Have you accepted Jesus Christ as Lord and Savior of your life?

Here's my story: I accepted Christ when I was in high school. One day at band practice, one of my fellow band mates asked me if I had been baptized. My response was "no." At that moment, he looked me straight in the eye and told me that I was going to hell if I didn't get baptized. Goodness I was frightened! I didn't get baptized immediately but one thing was for sure, I did not want to go to hell. (Around this same time, my family and I had just recently begun going to church regularly again.) Although I didn't know much about it, hell did not sound like some place I wanted to go. The more I thought about it, the more I began to wonder why **I** would have to go to hell. I was a pretty good kid. I earned good grades, I obeyed my parents, I was nice to people. After hearing so many good things about Jesus and this "new life" each Sunday, I made the decision to give my life to Christ and to get baptized as an outward representation that I accepted Christ.

As a young person, I thought that people would be able to look at me and "see" that I had accepted Christ. I thought that things on the outside would be different. However, as I matured in Christ, I have learned that I must first trust and allow God to change my heart. Change happened when I listened to what was being taught in church, read the bible and put into practice what I learned. I have learned that as I seek to grow closer to God, he draws closer to me. I have learned to seek Him in all things and rely on his power. Although I am not perfect, and do not always make the right choices, God is perfect. He is faithful, forgiving and merciful. My life with Him is much better than it would be without Him.

The word of God tells us in Romans 3:23 that everyone has sinned and fallen short of God's glorious standard. So "my goodness" was not enough to keep me from going to hell. No one is "good" enough. *Romans 3:25 NLT says "For God presented Jesus as the sacrifice for sin."* We are saved from eternal separation from God when we believe in our hearts and confess with our mouths that Jesus sacrificed his life, shedding his blood, for our sins.

Romans 10:9-10 NLT "If you confess with your mouth that Jesus is Lord and believe in your heart that God raised him from the dead, you will be saved. For it is by believing in your heart that you are made right with God, and it is by confessing with your mouth that you are saved."

Salvation Prayer: Lord God, thank you for sending your son Jesus to die on the cross for my sins. I recognize that I am a sinner and have fallen short of your glory. I believe that you sent Jesus to die for my sins and that you raised him from the dead. I ask forgiveness of my sins and believe that in this moment you have saved me and given me eternal life. In Jesus' name, Amen.

For further study, please read John 3:16, Romans 10:5-21 and Luke 23-24 in entirety.

Life Application

If you prayed this prayer for the first time, please find a church home to feed your faith and learn God's principles to living this earthly life. Life will not always be easy but now you have Christ to lean on. He will strengthen, comfort and guide you in ways beyond your imagination. Be encouraged, God loves you beyond measure.

Afterword

You have spent the last 30 days seeking the Lord's face and purpose for your life. I pray that you have received clarity and are empowered to do all of the great things that God has called you to do. Please review your journal and put your plans into action. Hopefully, consistently studying and reading God's word has become a habit for you over this past month and you continue to study, pray and write out your thoughts. Write down your plans. Write down what God places on your heart as you study your bible. God wants you to be all He has created you to be and you can only be that person if you know Him. You get to know God through His word.

Don't stop here. You have a lot of work to do. Begin by loving those around you the way that God intended. Learn to see others through His eyes. Remember: there is something within you that someone else needs. That "something" is part of your purpose. Someone is waiting on you to do what you have been called to do! When you release what's inside of you, you empower those around you. Others get to know God's love through you!

You live ***The Life Your Spirit Craves*** when you live the life that God has called you to live! Remember that your spirit craves to be like the Holy Spirit.

About the Author

Natasha was raised in Greenville, MS where she was spiritually nurtured under the leadership of Pastor Larry Benford, The Living Word Fellowship Church. Natasha currently resides in Missouri City, TX with her husband and daughter. Her family attends Higher Dimension Church under the leadership of Pastor Terrance Johnson. At Higher Dimension, Natasha has served as a member of the Finance and Higher Care ministries. She currently serves in the capacity of assisting her husband in his leadership duties for the intercessory prayer ministry. Natasha's passion is to encourage her peers to live the life of purpose that God has called them to live.

For more information about the author, please visit www.encouraging-works.com.